THE MAGIC OF
YELLOW

The Color Books are dedicated to the Rainbow Child in all of you

Series concept by Ayman Sawaf
Copyright © 1995 by Enchanté Publishing
MRS. MURGATROYD Character copyright © 1993 by Enchanté
MRS. MURGATROYD™ is a trademark of Enchanté

Written by Neysa Griffith.
Character created by Steven Duarte.
Illustrated by Deborah Morse.
Edited by Gudrun Höy and Anne Sheldon.

Enchanté Publishing
P.O. Box 620471
Woodside, CA 94062

Printed in Singapore

Library of Congress Cataloging-in-Publication Data
Griffith, Neysa
The magic of yellow / written by Neysa Griffith; character created by Steven Duarte; illustrated by Deborah Morse. - 1st ed.
      p.   cm.
Summary: Playful verses and illustrations invite children to enter the magical world of colors.
ISBN 1-56844-027-8 : $6.95
1. Yellow —Juvenile poetry. 2. Colors—Juvenile poetry.
3. Children's poetry. American [1. Yellow —Poetry. 2. American poetry.]
I. Neysa Griffith.   II. Morse, Deborah, ill.   III. Title.
PS3557.R4893M33   1994
811' .54—dc20   93-34812

First Edition
10 9 8 7 6 5 4 3 2 1

THE MAGIC OF
YELLOW

Written by Neysa Griffith
Illustrated by Deborah Morse

enchanté Publishing

Sunshine is the yellow blaze
of the warm and lazy summer days.
The canary sings a yellow song.
Yellow is laughter all day long.

Busy, buzzing bumblebees
float gently on the summer breeze.
Into daffodils they dive,
to gather pollen for their hive.

Their honey sweetens our lemonade
which we sip in cooling shade.

Yellow is joyous and yellow is fun,
a frolic in the noontime sun.
Running through the golden wheat,
the prairie flowers smell so sweet.

Yellow is happy and yellow is smart,
a smooth and creamy lemon tart.

A bright idea, a happy thought,
chamomile tea brewed up in a pot.

Yellow galoshes and yellow raincoats,
yellow school buses and yellow sailboats.

Yellow brings a cheerful morning.
Sometimes yellow means a warning.

Lightening bolts and fireflies
illuminate the darkest skies.
Yellow is the desire to know
ideas that make the light bulbs glow.

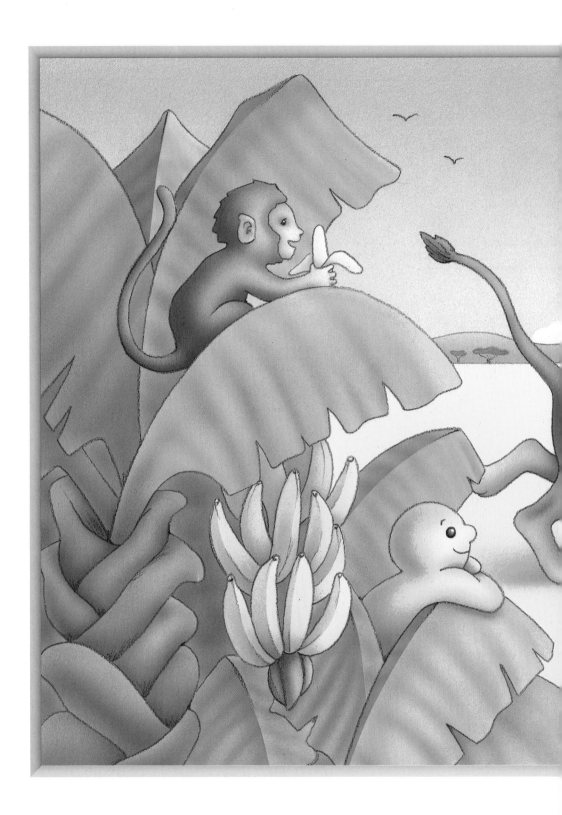

Yellow bananas picked from a bunch
make a hungry monkey's lunch.
The mighty lion likes to roam
the dry savannah of his home.

Yellow is the desert land
of pyramids and golden sand.
Sparkling stars light up the night.
A moon made of cheese shines
twice as bright.

With halo ring and golden wings,
a magic wishing angel brings
a pot of gold for you to share
with other children everywhere.

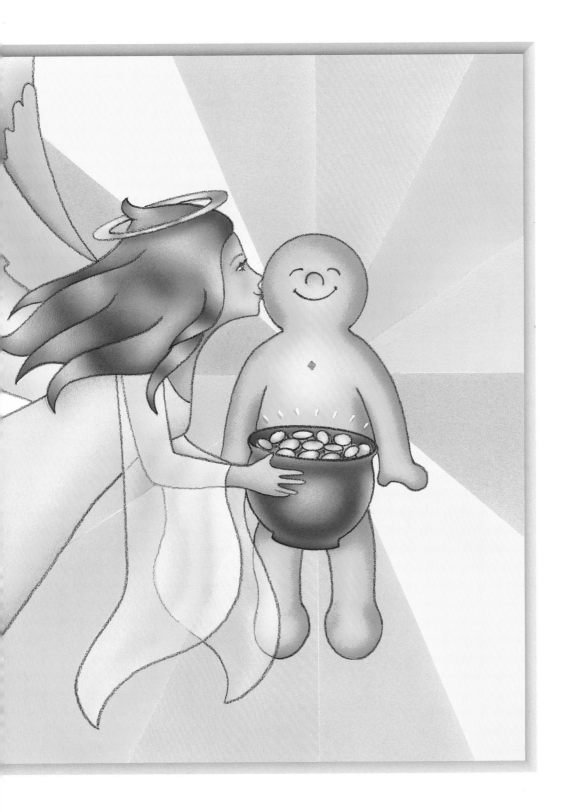

The magic of yellow is inside of you.
It can happily help you in all that you do.
To make yellow your friend,
close your eyes and pretend...

In a garden where you stand,
yellow flowers grace the land.

Daisies with smiles, sunflowers so tall,
you feel like a pixie who's three feet small.

A giant dandelion with a "pick me" sign
is covered in dream fluffs, soft and fine.
A wish will come true for each girl and boy.
Let your spirit fly free, and feel the joy!

Enchanté books are dedicated to enhancing the general well-being of children by encouraging them to use their own imagination and creativity to explore their thoughts and feelings. Each story is a symbolic journey into the magical world of self, where children discover the power they have within. Enchanté offers high quality hardcover picture books with accompanying activity books and parents' guides which include:

And Peter Said Goodbye
Exploring Grief
Exploring Grief With Your Child

Painting the Fire
Exploring Anger
Exploring Anger With Your Child

Red Poppies for a Little Bird
Exploring Guilt
Exploring Guilt With Your Child

The Rainbow Fields
Exploring Loneliness
Exploring Loneliness With Your Child

Nightmares in the Mist
Exploring Fear
Exploring Fear With Your Child

William's Gift
Exploring Hurt
Exploring Hurt With Your Child

Knight-time for Brigitte

For more information call:
1-800-473-2363
or (415) 529-2100
fax # (415) 851-2229

enchanté Publishing